PIANO • VOCAL • GUITAR

25 MODERN WORSHIP SONGS FOR A NEW GENERATION

W9-DEB-846

CONTENTS

ISBN 0-634-02156-7

HAL•LEONARD® CORPORATION

7777 W. BLUEMOUND RD. P.O. BOX 13819 MILWAUKEE, WI 53213

Visit Hal Leonard Online at
www.halleonard.com

BETTER IS ONE DAY

Words and Music by
MATT REDMAN

Moderately, with a strong beat

How love-ly is Your dwell-ing place,
thing I ask and I would seek:

O Lord Al-might - y, for my soul longs and
to see Your beau - ty, to find You in the

e - ven faints for You,
place Your glo - ry dwells.
for
One

THE HAPPY SONG

Words and Music by
MARTIN SMITH

Fast two-beat

Oh, I could sing un - end - ing
I could dance a thou - sand

songs of how You saved my soul. __

Well, I could dance a thou - sand miles be - cause of _____ Your great love. __

Oh, ev - 'ry - bod - y dance. *Instrumental solo - ad lib.*

Solo ends

COME, NOW IS THE TIME TO WORSHIP

Words and Music by
BRIAN DOERKSON

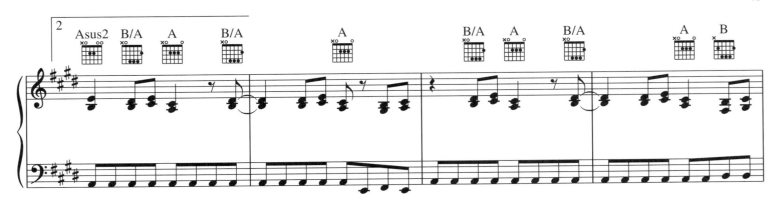

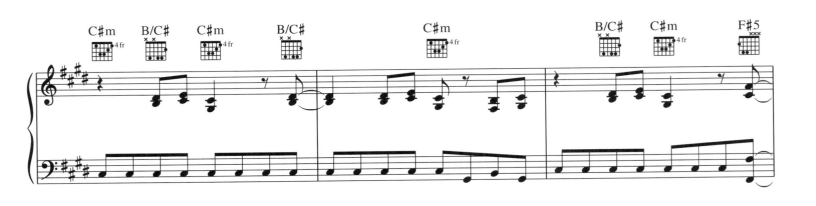

Ooh, _____

-ly choose _ You now. _

Spoken: One day.

DID YOU FEEL THE MOUNTAINS TREMBLE?

Words and Music by
MARTIN SMITH

EVERY MOVE I MAKE

Words and Music by
DAVID RUIS

Moderately, in 2

Ev - 'ry move I make, I make in You; You make me ___ move, Je - sus.

Ev - 'ry breath I take, I breathe in You. ___

Ev - 'ry step I take, I take in You; You are my ___ way, Je - sus.

Ev - 'ry breath I take, I breathe in You.

Waves of mer - cy, waves of grace, _____

THE HEART OF WORSHIP

Words and Music by
MATT REDMAN

I COULD SING OF YOUR LOVE FOREVER

Words and Music by
MARTIN SMITH

I WILL EXALT YOUR NAME

Words and Music by
JEFFREY B. SCOTT

JESUS, FRIEND OF SINNERS

Words and Music by
PAUL OAKLEY

Driving Rock

There is a voice ___ that must ___ be heard. ___
There is a peace ___ that calms ___ our fears. ___

There is a song ___ that must ___ be sung. ___   There is a name ___ that must ___
There is a love ___ strong - er ___ than death. ___   There is a hope ___ that goes ___

JESUS, LOVER OF MY SOUL

Words and Music by
PAUL OAKLEY

49

JOY

Words and Music by
JOHN ELLIS

Bright Rock

love You, Lord,   I   wor - ship You,   I
Lord, I   love   to   bring   to   You   the

LORD, REIGN IN ME

Words and Music by
BRENTON BROWN

POUR OUT YOUR SPIRIT

Words and Music by
TOM LANE

ONCE AGAIN

Words and Music by
MATT REDMAN

D.S. al Coda

CODA

OPEN THE EYES OF MY HEART

Words and Music by
PAUL BALOCHE

ho - ly, ho - ly, ho - ly. To see You

high and lift - ed up, shin -

- ing in the light of Your glo - ry.

SET ME ON FIRE

Words and Music by
RYAN DELMORE

Bright Rock

I am ___ so tired ___ of com - pro - mis -

SHOUT TO THE LORD

Words and Music by
DARLENE ZSCHECH

THANK YOU FOR THE BLOOD

Words and Music by
MATT REDMAN

SHOUT TO THE NORTH

Words and Music by
MARTIN SMITH

TRADING MY SORROWS

Words and Music by
DARRELL EVANS

sor - rows, _
sick - ness, _
I'm trad - ing _ my _
shame; _
pain; _

I'm lay - ing _ them down for the joy of _ the

Lord.

WE FALL DOWN

Words and Music by
CHRIS TOMLIN

WE WANT TO SEE JESUS LIFTED HIGH

Words and Music by
DOUG HORLEY

We want to see, we want to see, we want to see Je-

-sus lift-ed high. __ We want to see, we want to see,

we want to see Je - sus lift - ed high. __

To Coda ⊕

Step by

- sus lift - ed high. ___ We want to see, we want to see,

(clap)

we want to see Je - sus lift - ed high. ___ We want to see,

we want to see, we want to see Je - sus lift - ed high. _

(clap) *(clap)*

___ We want to see, we want to see, we want to see Je -

(clap)

WHAT A FRIEND I'VE FOUND

Words and Music by
MARTIN SMITH

Slowly and gently

Lyrics:

(1.) What a friend I've ___ found,
(2.,3.) What a hope I've ___ found,
more clos-er than a broth-er.
faith-ful than a moth-er.
I have felt Your ___ touch
It would break my ___ heart
more in-ti-mate than ___ lov-ers. }
to ev-er lose each ___ oth-er. }

YOU ARE MERCIFUL TO ME

Words and Music by
IAN WHITE

YOU'RE WORTHY OF MY PRAISE

Words and Music by
DAVID RUIS

And I will give __ You all my wor - ship.

8vb throughout